City Of Bridges

City Of Bridges

Jo Slade

salmonpoetry

Published in 2005 by
Salmon Publishing,
Cliffs of Moher, County Clare, Ireland
Website: www.salmonpoetry.com
email: info@salmonpoetry.com

ISBN 1 903392 46 2

Cover artwork: Jo Slade
Cover design: David Slade
Typesetting: Siobhán Hutson

Salmon Publishing gratefully acknowledges the financial support
of The Arts Council / An Chomhairle Ealaíon

For Susan Knighton

Acknowledgments

Grateful acknowledgment is made to the following publications in which some of these poems, or earlier versions of them, first appeared:

Certain Octobers, Bilingual Publication, Editions Eireanna, Quimper France 1997; *An Cloigeann is a Luach/What Worth the Head*, County Limerick Anthology 1998; *The White Page/An Bhileog Bhan: Twentieth Century Irish Women Poets*, Salmon Publishing, Galway, 1999; *Dandelion Literary Magazine*, University of Calgary, Canada 2000; *The Stoney Thursday Book*, Limerick 2001; *La Traductaire* Poetry Magazine, Paris France 2002; *The SHOp* Literary Magazine, Schull, Co. Cork 2003. *The Limerick Leader* 2003. *Poetry Ireland Review* No. 76 2003. *La Traductaire* Poetry Magazine, Paris, France 2003.

I wish to express my thanks to the Arts Council of Ireland for Travel Awards which supported this work.

Contents

I

What's That Snapping?

What's that snapping?
Before you know it
you're losing all sense of time.
It's snowing and you feel
the temperature drop.
You wish you were back
where you started or near an ending.

Either he was snapping dead
wood from the cherry tree or
she was breaking twigs for firewood.
That's how it happens in the memory
 you hear a sound and you're back there.

It used to be that there was a unity of things
the hill, the snow, the low buildings
down the valley, the cherry tree
kindling, them, me, the silence—
the creepy silence of snow.

Then you feel it like ice cracking
on your tongue.
You're back with the living
you're almost where you're heading.
That's how it happens in the memory
that's how it is. We never let them go.

Singspeil

My mother sang in the morning, in the afternoon
in the evening she sang for my father
and in the dark night when she couldn't be seen
she sang like Charlotte Delbo or Nina—
songs full of beauty and pain.

And I lay there—
afraid to let go of her sound, so familiar.
I longed to be near her, to hold her to feel her,
child of her opera of home.

PapaDa
(The Picasso Museum. August 1997.)

Love me Papa   Holy Papa happy.
Don't be a silver soldier with a spear.
Don't be a stranger.
Don't be a stray dog that follows
no matter where.

I Didn't Be—Myself

I didn't be—myself spake once twice
to name for each   fatherdaughter.
I can't remember
not to forget.
In Truth the name left
                                        scurried away...
Am afraid
of forgetting.

Seesaw as we were (two strangers)
walking talking. *I*
shall be a painter.
I'm getting [less and less] like Father.
Speak eyespeak.
Know your place, daughter.

I remember these hands
and his voice:
commandments.
Who say'th Father Lord Rabboni—
which book whose story
severally heard
passed on   word for word ?

Am difficult,
to find the wilderness of you.
Can't find the sound
am bound
wrist to heel by Love.

The Lesson

Rule of position: One
taken to begin.
Call this the right hand and the other,
left.
Try to remember which is which.
One child left
handed. Dismissed.

Try again—
hold your hands perpendicular.
One [right hand, little finger.]
One two three One two three.
One
        sun moon penis,
two
        hands breasts wings,
three
        love trembling...

What goes by the name of love
goes by the Name:
Eka Abja Indu Father.

Remember two   together
                    by the river
like flies trembling,
or yard cats screaming.
Then One again   or none.
Either.

Mother Licht

I ask you to come to me.
To come close as breath to me.
To hold me in that world of sea
and grass that belongs to me.

I do not insist that you stay with me—
but know that you remain close to me
even though you are no longer part of me.

A Curtain Of Chimes

A curtain of chimes
surround the beloved.
Touch the word *Father*
and the air is filled
with sunlight and longing.

Kinda Blue

i was you mamabluebabe singing
i was you the swoon
around the room
dolldreaming

dance mamablue
dance with your baby
dance in the blueheart
with papa going crazy.

i was you mamablueheartbreaking
singing you is me too
in the blue room of your making
in the blue house faking.

Sing mamablue
when the heart breaks open
i will sing for you too
mamabluebabe's singing.

I Was Waiting Under the Bridge

I was waiting under the bridge,
the old bridge at the edge of my city.
Imagine how dark I felt—
dark as the river that was inside me.

I was waiting beneath the wings
of the angel of my city
beside the Romanesque church
near the river of rain.

I was waiting as if he would come
through the rain to see me.
As if he would take my arms and lift me
immerse me in cloud
like the angel of Cevennes.

I was waiting at the corner
where four roads cross over.
I thought I would meet him coming home
the smell of clouds on his hands.

Little stone night,
night of sapphires and spires
of something resisting in the city
and on pavements where I stood
in the evening,
on the last day of his life.

You Think I Have Something To Give

"You think I have something to give"
I show you my giving
I show it to you in truth and you turn away
as the sun turns from the living.

"You think I have something to give"
you think I am solemn.
In my love there is solemnity—
in my love there are intricacies.

I am here and the wren and the swallow
we are here at the intersection
and we wait—
we wait in serenity, with nothing.

After Picking

Smokehouse apples in a bucket.
Things occur and pass away.
My Da said, *"it's a story,"*
he called it mysterious
the way appleblossom appears
even in snow.
It comes just as quick as it goes.

The apples in our orchard were different.
Beautiful they were, red and golden
and crisp as dry timber
sweet as honey on our fingers.
Sometimes I think he's here with us,
sitting under the silver maple
his head slung back casual
as if he'd like to stay.

Three buckets and a crimson moon.
Sometimes, if I see too clearly
if light changes those strange transparencies
I lose him again and again.
Every autumn it's the same story
of loss and gain,
of eyes full of apples red and golden
and noisy buckets full of rain.

Mother—Elder

For Jenny

"And where is Mother—Elder ?
She is in the tea-pot," her mother said,
"and there let her remain."

Now distracted in her concern, she sat upon the cold stone
and saying her evening prayersong, quiet, so the wind
    would hear her
she began with fingers crossed to create her word music.
And so she visited in her mind places stored from dreams.
The moon seemed almost edgeless in its blur
and there were nightbirds, did you see them free as choppers
from a tree spinning, did you get inside their feelings flying?
"Hurrah now we'll ride many miles away."

So she crept upon the lowest ground and found it to be soft.
"It is beautiful here in winter" trees are white with frost
and all the sky is seamless, soundless,
you follow through as if close to a dream.

These words, not music, now she considers
but holds the moon close to her, like coral white or brimstone
and sorrow tight inside the heart, tight enough to choke.
The moon will surely spill its liquid silver thus and fill me full.
"It is beautiful here in spring" the forest sings alive all things
new and particular in their wonder.
Mother—Elder, older tree, find me when I wander,
sing the songs that we remember.

"It is delightful here in summer" the fields you'll find
are softest carpets and sun inside rivers warm
and ditches, yellow flowers and painters to catch
like wisps colours drift or underfoot

the sensual feet in grasses too numerous to number.
Rare things, spare, nought, almost there
perhaps part of her yearning for her fields,
the perfumed air, never to be forgotten.
"It is delightful here in autumn."

Catch that cool breeze as it leaves the mountain
lonely dipped in upon the sea it changes nearly to crimson
such is the same for certain shells that appear dull as ditch
in air but sparkle when they breath inside the water.
Mother—Elder turns to gold and paints like Hisho-Mi
with thin brush words least spoken, uttered, thrown
on the world and dissolved before first frost freeze
Mother—Elder calls a daughter loved one.
Only seeming quiet the seed beneath
and the girlchild grew.
Whilst others call her Dryad,
she is, touch her, so does she outlive the life
and call upon you sweetness child.
Remember, what falls inside the forest heart she sees.

White Bird

In my dream you were a bird of grace and beauty.
A luminous, magical bird, estranged from the world.

You flew in and out of the sleeping bridge
where the spirit of my city plays in water,
you spread your wings across the river
and a thousand kisses rose from the dust of streets.

In a circle of space beside trees my dream faltered.
Trees that cannot be reached,
that are part of the starry universe.

Words sleep in the drift and light, they turn over
in their small place, secluded in vacuoles of air.
Sounds float back, oriole of my dream that night—
white bird caught in midair mesmerised by water.

I Know Where To Find You

I know where to find you
if I want to find you
if you want to be here.
It's clear on a plane night
on a night of pitch and flight
where to find you.

All preservations contain you:
liquefied, calcified, crystalised.
If you want to be here
with heat over you
and on trees in the garden of the holy.

Returning.Out of the shade
and bouyancy in the fountain
In dreams of the lonely at that time of evening
when I know where to find you.
If you want to be here
peripheral, between journeys.

So this is how we leave,if we leave,finally.
Lost in transparency or petrified to stone—
a shale of rock crumbling
or the sound of bees swarming in the oak.
Still, you know where to find me
if you want to find me—
if I want to be found.

Let The Body Go

I hear you in my deep sleep
leaving
and the dance drum beating
letting go.
The prayer: To Leave
and leaving to go.

Enough of loss is never past.
Never truly known
the Go...ing.
Never truly known
the woman   letting go.

Dying to float
the old woman in her bodyboat.
Leaving

blind as ice
cold as crow feet on a frozen lake.
A waste
of bodybones slip away.

Let go...
the freezing pain. Slow
slowing down
the breath it takes to Be.

Before going
one last taste of skin.
Slip the fish-head in
suck the roe.
Let them know   you're leaving.

Dying
to slip the sleeplatch
to let the body go.

Fatherhand

If you say it slowly,
say for instance *morning*—
say, *the dawn unfolding*
and seeing through the haze
a man approaching,

his white hair exactly as you recall—
a fall of silver leaves picked
from the snowtree in his garden.

Say you hide, holding the breath inside
afraid to brush
against his passing,
barely breathing—

you're a foxchild sniffing the dark thorns
treading the forest floor in fear of shadows.
He emerges—
all glint and gust to pick you up.

You weep then in deepest space—
tethered by the father hand
homed inside the father land.

The Grey Wolf Day

The grey-wolf day is leaving.
Curiously, their eyes blossom
like sprays of lilies.

Everywhere I look I see
tinges of truth.
In the sky, in the white spruce
of this wilderness.

Bright sun—
the austral summer in December.
Doves carry them like feathers
until they disappear.

Such calculation
tracing the precision of loss.
If I return to their house
it is without the usual emotion.

What Do We Become?

What do we become,
after long intervals ?

Days and evenings hung
with candles
and light balm
and the wind.
The barbed explication
of noon
and the distance—
how far to you?

Your hands reappear.
At that second — present
when hands resume

their secret meeting
we become, like noon.

Obedience

I think I have reached the end
of obedience.
I have seen it out on the lake
with the sail of my heart
keeping it afloat.

It was so long to be without
my will to guide me.
When I walk in the autumn garden
I think in single words—
Wind, Bridge, Motion,
a mapping occurs.
One by one the beat
of my heart is returning.

II

Crossings

You see too much
that is why the treachery of crossings
inhibits you.

Look—
the bridge is certainly wide enough
and utterly luminous.

An immense silence fills you.

It spreads through your city
it enters the river
it turns in a glow of moon.

In a scent of winter the heart breaks.
Then a swirl of emptiness—
like gusts of memory inside a ruin.

Colour Photographs

What do you see on their faces ?
Blood is on their faces and in their eyes.
The blood of the bull on their faces
and their own blood and my blood
on the four matadors.

Yesterday in a pink coat
with gold buttons and laces.
Today in a red coat
tomorrow in a cream coat.
Embroidered caps and blood
from the bull on their faces
and my blood on their coats
and in their eyes
the four matadors.

In the streets they sing for him.
One is strong to slay the bull.
One innocent to beguile him.
One will die in him.
A red tie for poppies that waver
a yellow bolero for trees in the meadow
for the blood of the bull
on their faces and in their eyes
the four matadors.

Semana Santa / Andalusia

For Pauline Goggin

Our Lady of Loneliness, Our Lady of the Red Earth
Mother of the Pure and the Impure Mother of Sorrows
Virgin of the Moon and the Stars
Black Virgin of the Sea in her winter house facing the storm
in her white church that rocks like a boat—
shelter for women who cannot grow old
shelter for sisters and talk of sisters.

Black Virgin of the Waves in her summer home
at the foot of the mountain.
Protection for strangers and the goatherd.
Compassion for the black pig who grazes
in the shade of the jacaranda.
Pity for women who have sons and daughters
and for women who don't.
Bless them with stars that dance on the water.
Tenderness for children. *Todas los besos.*

Songs for men who smell of the horse, *Toda mi fuerza.*
Prayer for the bull who remembers his daughters
and refuses to die, for his heart that beats into the night
and penetrates the joy of the crowd, that isn't joy
but fear of joy. Pity for bulls on the camino de tauro.
Pity for men who follow men.

Virgin of Gardens, Our Lady of Blood
is the poinsettia tree in spring. Prayer for women who bleed.
Our Lady of Squalor Mother of Perpetual Help
Virgin of Horror swathed in snow. Mother of the Blind
Daughter to Anna, Virgin of the Unbound
Star of the Sea who is guide to the Father, remember me.

Our Lady of the Rocks in her dark cave under the earth
in her white shift smelling of dust—*toda mi muerte.*
Mother of all Deaths—Remember us.

* *Todas los besos / Toda mi fuerza / toda mi muerta (All the kisses / All my
strength / all my deaths).*

A Garden In Tuscany

For Janet Mularney

"...when the eye becomes audible."
    Edmond Jabes

Time of cypresses in low mist,
time of lemons, moment by moment into yellowness.
Time of ecstasy, a garden of fantasy
a scent of woodsmoke and leaves.

Time of the urn and a glove by the pool in the half-light
his voice like a bell from the balcony.
Surrounded by larkspur, love-in-a-mist,
windflower, wood anemone.

Time to retrieve whatever is left—
echoes of a Bach piece blown through a room,
pale clouds over a field.
A scent of jasmine, a cobalt sky.

I remember light fading and grass pale
under a white moon,
the sound of night birds feeding
and warm air rising in a blue room.

City Of Bridges

I will tell you....
over each bridge I threw
something I owned.

First my kid gloves.
Then a silk scarf,
precious to me since
it bore the print of my love.
Then a white flower
(it had just been given to me.)
And my black dress
and my boots zipped at the ankle
and my tights—
so sheer you would think them
my soul and its shade.

As if it were yesterday...
these pieces of myself afloat.
My dress filled like a scoop
my boots sad descent
so quick, so quiet.
And the white flower caught
in a cusp of river dirt.
And my gloves,
my own hands gold
so gold you would think them caskets
of air caught in a glint of sunlight
or wings of a rare bird that ride the swell.

I will tell you,
at each bridge I rid myself of something.
I was ...becoming weightless
spare, detached, pared down
nothing to bear.

Pegasus Bridge Benoville France 9/7/99

You.   You who are passing....

My father crossed this bridge on the way to Ranville
on D-Day.
What is amazing is ..."

What was it ? I mean, what it meant in the End
                              is
we are free.

What is amazing is...the way stars reappear.
The same hemisphere.The same North declination.

Myth says,*"His hoof hit the ground
and a fountain sprung forth."*

So much blood resurgent.

Freedom meant not being a slave, a prisoner.

Now, the sound of traffic crossing.
A constant clip clump.

Hart called it, *The Full Ebb. The Spread. The Turn.*
What he meant was: The sun fell on a town.
                          Everything burned.
                          80,000 burnt into the ground.

In the End. Immolation.

Prague 1998

As if a purple cloud descended
and filled my throat—
lilacs bloom above the city.

Like a child I watch for you.
More than anything
I want to see you in your black beret
and fur gloves.
More than anything
I want to hear you call across to me.

I sit by Saint's Bridge—
the cold is almost unbearable.
Yet, everywhere I look
trees are starting to bloom
and the air fills with perfume of lilac...

Spring

On winter nights I sleep naked
on our bed.
Wrapped between snowfalls,
the last of winter, the first of spring
I remember him
slipping into me,
arched beneath me
his craned head lithe
as a swan's reflection on the riverbed.

June

The lights and darks of summer.
Trees edge the field like soft pillows
you could disappear into,
the silent river gems a silver glow.
Everywhere I look I feel the same breeze
that moves inside the grass and makes it whisper.

Nothing is changed—
except in winter when I walk here
the shy birch hums its loss and last leaves are spread
like small deaths in the snow.

Troposhere

Sometimes a storm comes as muddy ochres.
Sometimes a storm springs out of cloud banks
earth browns, sharp as shit against snow.

When I saw the deep blue brown coming,
fierce as a boxer entering the ring
I knew I'd never let him go,

that he'd always be there, in the murkiness
and I'd always be watching the sky
the quality of light
that slow time before a storm.
The space between silence and letting go.

Wind

The apple forgets the dream of wind
it forgets the tree and how last spring
it was a beautiful blossom.

It forgets the east wind that entered
the garden, like Vanya's ghost.
The apple remembers nothing,

not a feeling of sweetness nor being
being touched by wind and drifting—
leaves shimmering in the late autumn light.

The Rain Is Falling

The rain is falling
the song bird is weeping.
Listen.
The pine has a song
and the oak another.

Rain falls
through our fingers
and on our faces
and on leaves
that have fallen.

Pure Direction

Little forest of my own will—
how free are you ?

This morning—
how free are you ?

The goose who flies
through air is free.
Wings are everything.

Wings are better than a soul—
flight is greater than imagination.

Look. The goose knows where he goes.
He understands pure direction.

What Do You Love?

What do you love?
Is it the frail flower
that leans to kiss you.

Is it the sharp thorn
that grows unaware
of its own fierce sting.

Or is it that love itself
inhabits you and so
as though you were a rose

I reach to touch you
and feel in my desire
that you have pierced my skin?

10 Easy Pieces

A Good Morning Melody

In every human life
there is morning—
the chemistry of seasons
the dripping of dew.
There is nothing
that we might not lose—
except love.

Meditation

Now you can't say
which means more to you.
Either you are the same
as the gypsywoman
or you carry woodsacks
back and forth to the stream.
Whichever, it makes no difference.
Either way
the mark of your feet will be seen.

To See More

You wonder , how goes life with the hawk—
what does she see
stars, snow on the mountain, a phantom,
her own shape in the stream.
Who knows ?
She sees what she wants to see.

Talking To Myself

Fishergirl where is your casket ?
If you lose it
a cold wind will inhabit you
and your corpse
will shine like glass
and your golden hair
will burn
between ten thousand stars.

The Art of Flying

I have reduced myself   slightly
to a star
a perfect planet   a plane
projection on a Blue ocean
a blaze of fire.

About Passing...

The train speeds on
and long
after this a hand is waving—
say to the child
"Stop Waving"
say to the eager hand
"It is gone."

Farewell

The shadow cast
on my palm
clung to my forehead.
I should look up.
You should be there.
You are not.

A Tune a Day

Do you remember what you used to believe
and where you lived,
in a house carved from pine and cedar.

Do you remember in winter the sun dropped
among trees and you dragged it behind you
and hung it on the west wall until spring ?

Greetings from Pamalican

Two women who are good friends
join the silence of the planets.
They appear like abandoned spirits
who float high above the world.
These women are older than stars.
They are closer than skin
to the hair of a rabbit.

A Good Night Melody

My brother says his dreams
are of Parmenides, the old man.

Now nothing can change.
Not for him.

*The titles and inspiration for these poems are from
Zbigniew Preisner's *'10 Easy Pieces for Piano'*. EMI Classics 2000.

Poetry

Inside my eye
at the blackest point I dream
like a freechild or a redwing
or the spirit of a fox
just released by hounds.

Because I am so small
you could tread on me.
You could laugh at my fear
and I could not defend me.

That is how I learned
to curl into a ball,
to hand over all I own
except one thing
that is a gift to me.

Because I am so small
life could devour me.
At Easter I take my gift
to the tallest tree—
so it grows strong to defend me.

The Tale Of The Poor Poet

For Clairr O'Connor

Today my basket is empty.
So it is that I go to the market—
not to buy, since I have no money
but to pick off the road
those bits that have fallen,
been discarded.

As I am third child in a family
and an old woman
I recognise the cunning ways
of people. How they procure
the tenderest fruit
how they fill their baskets with eggs
and not one breaks.

How they steal from stalls
with soft hands and white teeth
and how they mix convivially—
calling each by their first name.
How pretty are their children

who speak a high grammar
with sixteen words to describe feet
and many difficult sounds
for God or godliness.
I see how they eat, always ravenous
they fill their mouths
with sweet cake and roast meat.

My friend wears a grey coat
she is guard at the outer gate.
She loves me so she hides her face

when I approach—
that way it is no fault for her
if the poor crawl through streets
with no words and empty baskets.

My home is a frail shed, I keep out
wind and rain with old sheets.
I have a blanket of blue wool
this is how I never feel chilled—
this is how I dream
not of baskets heavy with eggs or fruit,

not of sixteen words to describe feet
but of the orange blossom that grew
sometime ago in my memory.
When warm winds blow from the east
you will notice my flower—
this blossom that sleeps deep in my mind.

Love Vessel

For Richard

What if I could make a vessel for you.
A pot simple in shape, in blue majolica shades.
So subtle they would look at it and say
I had pulled it from the sea.

What if one day you grew into my vessel.
Your blood spread round the very tip
The way I'd paint delicate lips on a portrait head.

Then by some twist of fate, I might drink from you.
Sip you sweet my love.
Become what I should be, conduit of love's wisdom.

Notes

Singspeil: Charlotte Delbo, French writer and poet.
A survivor of Auschwitz prison camp.
Nina Simone, jazz and blues singer.

I Didn't Be—Myself: Title taken from Emily Dickinson,
The Master Letters. Lines in italics from
Van Gogh Letters.

The Lesson: Line in italics from Samuel Beckett's,
First Love.

You Think I Have Something to Give:
Title taken from, Simone Weil, *Letters to
Her Mother 1943.*

Mother—Elder: Loosely based on the fairy tale, *Mother—Elder*
by Hans Anderson.

Let the Body Go: Line in italics from Samuel Beckett's, *First Love.*

Colour Photographs: Photographs by Rineke Dijkstra 1994.

Pegasus Bridge: Inspired by a postcard from a friend. Lines
1, 2 & 15 are quoted from that postcard.

10 Easy Pieces: Titles are taken from Zbigniew Preisner's,
10 Easy Pieces for Piano. EMI Classics 2000.